Tabby in the tree

Story by Beverley Randell
Illustrated by Julian Bruere

A big dog came
into Kate Green's garden.
It saw Tabby the cat.
"Woof! Woof! Woof!"

Tabby ran to a tree.
She did not like dogs.

Tabby climbed up the tree.
"Woof! Woof!" went the dog.

Tabby went on climbing.
She climbed up
to the top of the tree.
"Meow," she said.

Kate Green ran into the garden to help Tabby.

"Go away!" she said to the dog.

"Go away! Go on, **go**!"

The dog went.

"Meow," said Tabby, up in the tree.

"Come down, Tabby.
The dog has gone now.
Come down to me,"
said Kate.

But Tabby stayed up
at the top of the tree.
"Meow," she said.

Kate got a ladder.
She climbed up to get Tabby.
"Come down, Tabby," she said.
"I'm here. Kitty, Kitty, Kitty."

But Tabby stayed up
at the top of the tree.
"Meow," she said.

Kate went inside.

"Let me see," she said.

"Tabby likes fish.

Will she smell it?

Will she come down

to get some fish?"

"Kitty, Kitty, Kitty," said Kate.
"Come on, Tabby. Here you are.
Can you smell the fish?
Come and get it,"
said Kate.

Tabby **did** smell the fish.

And down she came!
"Meow," said Tabby.